DUST LIGHT, LEAVES

DUST LIGHT, LEAVES

Christopher Buckley

VANDERBILT UNIVERSITY PRESS

Printed by Thomson-Shore, Inc., Dexter, Michigan

(handwritten) 00547 75330

The author and publisher make grateful acknowledgment to the editors of the following periodicals for permission to reprint those poems in this collection that first appeared in their publications:

"Quotidiana" Copyright © 1983 by the Antioch Review, Inc. First appeared in *The Antioch Review*, Vol. 41, No. 4 (Fall, 1983). Reprinted by permission of the Editors.

"Zurbaran's 'Still Life: Lemons, Oranges And A Rose' 1633"first appeared in *The Hudson Review*.

"For A Friend Lacking Faith" originally appeared in the Fall 1985 issue of *The Pennsylvania Review*.

"Prayer" and "Insomnia" were originally published in the Fall 1982 (Vol. 9, No. 1) issue of *Black Warrior Review*.

"Memory" and "Heaven Knows" were originally published in *Crazyhorse*.

"Lost and Found" originally appeared in the Spring 1983 issue (#16) of *Quarterly West*.

"La Strada" and "Spring And The Half Life" were first published in the Fall 1984 (Vol. XIV, No. 2) issue of *The Seneca Review*.

"Poem On A Birthday" first appeared in the Spring 1986 issue (#27/28) of *Three Rivers Poetry Journal*.

"Intransitive," "Work & Days," and "The Roadrunner" were first published in *The Missouri Review 1984-1985*.

"As It Is" was first published in the Spring 1982 (Volume 1, # 2) issue of *Cumberland Poetry Review*.

"Dust Light, Leaves" was first published in *The Georgia Review*.

"Smoke" and "Diffidence" were first published in the Spring 1980 issue of *Antaeus*.

"Mesopotamia" was first published in *The Reaper*.

"Why I'm In Favor Of A Nuclear Freeze" was first published in the Winter 1984 (Vol. 3, No. 1) issue of *Telescope* and copyrighted by The Galileo Press.

"Sparrows" was first published in the Spring 1982 (Vol. 1, No. 2) issue of *New Jersey Poetry Journal*.

"In The Rain Easing" originally appeared in *New England Review and Bread Loaf Quarterly*.

"Munch's 'Harvesting Women' " first appeared in the Winter 1982 (Vol. XC, No. 1) issue of *The Sewanee Review*.

The author wishes to add these special acknowledgments to:

Bieler Press for a limited edition chapbook of "Five Small Meditations on Summer and Birds"

The Anthology of Magazine Verse & Yearbook of American Poetry: 1985 for "Dust Light, Leaves"

Greenhouse Review Press for a limited edition broadside of "Post Card From Italy"

Pushcart Prize X for "Why I'm In Favor Of A Nuclear Freeze"

The National Endowment for the Arts for a grant in poetry for 1984 that enabled him to write many of these poems

Library of Congress Cataloging-in-Publication Data

Buckley, Christopher, 1948-
   Dust light, leaves.
   I. Title.
PS3552.U339D8   1986   811'.54   86-4081
ISBN 0-8265-1215-1 cloth
ISBN 0-8265-1219-4 paper

CONTENTS

I

Intransitive

Evening is that old tune I never tire of
especially when, as now, it is an adagio
of rose and grey above the autumn trees
and the turning leaves are nothing more
than brown and dead across the lawns.

When I was six or seven and climbed
the eucalyptus, or the pines,
I was in love, and wondering
at the underlay of music and everything
equally unattainable in the light—
I gave in to longing then, and liked it.

Doubtless, I have as much now as then—
and there is nothing less in an on-shore breeze
riffling the agapanthus and blue hibiscus,
or in the little salt on the air
lifting my lungs to breathe
as simple as that old desire to float
to where clouds turn red and dim,
to where the past dies out of us, and sleeps.

But this evening as I took the footpath
back up the long hill to the house,
I noticed the first few stars glide out
overhead and sing, and they were in need
of nothing more to complete their meaning.

                              for Deb & Edith Wylder

Lost And Found

for Kathy

Falling stars . . . silver spray
of the sprinkler across the lean
summer lawn, and I look up
to where the limbs of tamarisks
tangle toward space,
where a month ago
the stars were gone,
where now they line up and unlock
a little—the light currents
washing down the west . . .

I remember the road
along the shore, one of many moons
blooming in the top of a tall pine . . .
Tonight, above the salted cliffs,
beneath that tree, I think
two shadows must still love
in the lost arms of youth
and look out to stars,
to the bound spokes
of their wheel and long
for their lives like something
bright and shining toward them
as purely as the white sea stones
giving back their old desire
for the moon . . .

And now after all
the pollen from the fields
has been lifted in the wind
and let fall, after the chalk
has sifted down the buildings
in the cities of our past,
after the bruised wine
has been thrown from the cup
into the dust, and, in the harbor,
the lemon-colored sailing boats,
save one or two have left,

I will ignore the nightbird
insisting from the grove,
no life but this one,
and be grateful as the eucalyptus trees
for a late breeze and a chance
to take up an old song
and say this, my first love poem,
only to you, as if love were simply
misplaced among the skies,
a pause between stars, something
half-lost re-entering this world,
a meteor and its fiery hem,
first memory burning in the dark . . .

Mesopotamia

Since the Sumerians thought punishments were received only in this life and not in the next, they were interested mainly in living this life well.

—*from*
a Catholic High School *World History* text, © 1953

1956, and the world's as simple
as it's ever going to be . . .
My first uniform shirts are white
and our milk is delivered
by dairy trucks from Golden State.
Paper caps blow off the bottles
and I chase them down our drive
like scraps fallen from clouds.
I've memorized my first phone number—
92078—and can run the streets until
I'm called in for dinner or the dark.
I live on Humphrey Road and know
where it disappears into the maze
of bungalows and blue roofs
at the MiraMar Hotel, where lantana
and banana palms line a boardwalk.
I am also expert at identifying cars:
the sailfish fins of the '57 Chevy,
a Buick's grille with its thick grin,
the deluxe chrome of a Coupe de Ville.

At school, baseball is important
and we rip the knees out of our blue
parochial cords sliding into home.
I like trading the cards, and,
since I can't get a Stan Musial,
Brooklyn's Charlie Neal becomes
my favorite, though Santa Barbara
is a long way from where they play,
and no blacks attend our school.
This is the summer I will lose
my father's professional fielder's glove
when I leave it by the big ash tree
and ride bikes away with friends—
his disappointment builds in the house
like a sky going to rain; he just knew
I shouldn't have been trusted . . .

Nevertheless, the moon and clouds
are white and safe above me; I'm counting
nothing in the long grasses, listening
for the Southern Pacific "Daylight"
blaring by at 4:15, after which
we search the track for pennies
left there to be rolled leaf-thin.
The line curves along the seacoast
where below life blooms and scuttles
off beneath tidepool rocks, where
the world remains wide and slow
to come undone in our wondering hands;
but we can't care less, having come
this far on our own best guesses,
broad daylight and the advice of birds.

Mostly, I know about clouds—
feel my heart equally full, pure
and untethered—then one evening,
tuning in Ed Sullivan, a bulletin
interrupts with the Russians launching
a Sputnik into orbit. And this,
though I barely understand what's said,
though they have it looking like
a baseball stuck with soda straws,
is one more reason for my father
to have told us so, to stay
at the station and worry endlessly
over a newswire and unconscious world . . .

And he reads somewhere of a kid
who tries to fly out a window,
so after school I am forbidden
"Superman," which I watch anyway
never confusing myself with birds,
never forgetting my part in gravity.
Next year, I write my first poem—
Sr. Julie has us making cards
for Mother's Day and drawing around
the wedge-shaped print of our wishes.
In ten years I will come across it
in her cedar chest and be amazed
by four quatrains and exact rhymes
about sky-blue light and flowers in May,
all enhanced by two salt-white clouds

balanced perfectly above something yellow
blooming at the bottom of the page,
and indeterminate birds singing
from their enlarged and violet hearts.

Mainly this year, I enjoy the playoff
between the Dodgers and Milwaukee Braves.
Eddie Mathews is from our town
and he, Adcock, and Aaron score;
Lou Burdette turns a triple play.
We're the last kids with our mits
threaded on bike handles every day,
the last ones playing work-ups
long after school, until one Spring
someone is in love with Linda Underwood
or Maggie Tappenier—you take a walk
behind the buildings, something about
a St. Christopher's medal, getting kissed—
it lasts about a week and what do I know?
I know the difference between
the lemon blossom and the orange
riding the on-shore breeze, the fuchsia
that twirls like a ballerina in wind
or in my hand, which wild mustard
and nasturtium to eat, when loquats
will nod over the fence full of the sun's
orange sugar, and I'm not telling . . .

One evening after dinner, Seth Hammond
and I race to the steep grade where
the overpass for the 101 freeway will go;
we pull up the tall stakes trailing
red surveyors ribbons and throw them
for all we're worth toward the shadows
wavering in the down-wind light,
as if we are Romans or Greeks, someone
about whom we know something splendid
or noble, and not as if we were
6th graders with new math and drills
to duck & cover beneath our desks
from nothing we can see or make sense of.
I am making As in Social Studies and know
well that the earth is no longer round
or as large as we thought; I know
that a plane can drop through

the fine blue climate of Geography
and I could step out in Uruguay,
the sunny vista of Monte Video,
to admire the sailing boats starched
as table napkins down the River Plata . . .
And despite the unremembered history
of the Etruscans, or the Maya who left
their white cities and walked off into the blue,
a significant life was still possible—
for at this very moment any of us
could be breathing the same atoms of air
as Homer or Michelangelo, Parmenides
or Galileo, even some ordinary Sumerian
who, though the armies of the east
were on their way with iron and fire,
was overcome by nothing more than evening
releasing its terra cotta light
above the mists of two green rivers,
and so set down a bird-sure ode
to the easy waters and saffron clouds,
feeling there would never be a better time.

for Nadya

Memory

Saturday, another low spate of fog
tangles in the fruit trees, in the cold
outcroppings of rock up the hill
and another day finds me wanting
little more than the simple reasoning
of the sun, its quiet tides thinning
toward a day as unknown
as these late autumn leaves turning
slowly to light, and forgetting
their one green dream of life . . .

Some days I cannot stand to watch
another leaf blown loose across the lawn,
gathered, then turned to smoke,
to that last vague sentence of the past.

Maybe some things should be lost,
given the way the breeze
off the citrus groves suggests
the absent fragrance of love's oiled skin,
given these pebbles in the thin pocket
of the soul . . .
                    I don't know what
we're waiting for, though yesterday,
looking out the window in the 4:00 glare,
I saw a little band in red faded coats
with gold brocade, tall hats, tubas
and cornets—and the piccolo's melody
was a white flower of sorts carried
into the umber wave of a summer field,
and for a moment I was content with something
that was never my life at all . . .

Home, I walked out back to the open field
and there was only the day struggling across
the grass, the air a bright hovering dust.

Perhaps you've been there as well, and seen
the broken hands of light, the dry trees,
and felt for your own desire like some
stone too far down in an ice-cold stream?
Whatever there is to say about our loves,
it is not much, but how often we say it,
pointing a little more to what we want . . .

One day the rain eases and the air clears
so you can detail the mountains
you've only half looked at most your life—
you realize you love the sandstone
shrugged broadly at the top,
that you've always loved those few
weak veins of pines, the sky in back
turning white and thoughtless . . .

Crows circle and go on renouncing the world,
and of course God hears them too . . .
The seminary bell each morning reminds us
how we accept the silences drifting down to us
and how we each are, in the circumstances
of our ribs and skin, thin clay bells
begging a little something from the wind.

In The Rain Easing

For my grandfather, for Phil

No one believes that to die
is beautiful . . .
                        —*Levine*

One afternoon, I'm nine
sitting in the chicken yard,
keeping my own company, ready
to follow the redbird
over the big Ohio,
or down the roads of rusty clay,
believing that, like the hollyhocks
and pear leaves scurrying in the dust,
I will find my way back . . .
I might have been puzzling at
my voice flung far on a dark wind
or the unreadable intentions of light,
the singular grey flower of it closing
on the eastern sky . . . I was watching
the bruise-colored clouds
line the horizon and remembering
mother telling of tramps
leaving a mark by the drive,
turning up one after the other
to beg biscuits and supper . . .

I was digging
where I'd found marbles
rolled thirty years before
from my uncles' hands,
when grandmother bustled out of the kitchen,
her white dress going dull with rain,
the tiny pink roses turning dark . . .

Rain through dinner and then
the two long and one short rings
of our phone . . . and from the back
of my aunt's black Pontiac,
car lights coming on early
up the road to Elizabethtown,
and for the first time
I felt that vague absence
like light held off by clouds—
only nine and some seed of ash
taken hold in my chest . . .

I thought I knew what I knew . . .
that grandfather could peel the apple
in one perfect spiral—the world
just that easy for him—
I knew the guinea hens squawked
all day for not a damn thing,
that a man here swore, bit his lip
or spit in affirmation of the truth,
silent to his own pains . . .

And so my cousin and I sat quiet
in the hospital lot, car windows fogged,
until they came and hurried us in
where, in a transparent tent,
the sweat beaded on his forehead
like a rare and temperamental flower . . .

In two days mother and I were headed west
and what there was inside us wasn't much—
the farm's washed-out fields,
the faces of relatives in a grey
procession down the hill,
ashes, the songs, the wind . . .

So it was that some twenty years later
when the first one my age slipped off
the thin shirt of his life
no more than his car's handful of sparks
along a road where clouds had been gathering
for years, no more than the one spark
of the heart failing, I again tossed
as easily as a new leaf in storm,
feeling the rain's cold hands,
the lake of last words filling . . .

Today, when a spring shower caught me
midway jogging to the beach, I watched
the headlamps of the cars blur
in the distance of 3:00, and was stopped
recalling all this . . . and then later,
taking down a book, I noticed
that dash after the year of your birth,
and understood something I'm not sure
I want to . . . 30 years ago you wanted to be

someone with books, a name
and now already you're there—
the words waiting to flood out
into that dark sea of patience . . .

I think of how your hair's grizzled,
how over Spanish wine under the elms
we all complained of keeping
the body and the heart in shape.
By 50 you learned to praise the apple
and pass a little on the drink,
knowing the rush of all the wings
untied in the blood—you held out your hand
and when you waited, starlight
and the lemon blossoms on the air,
the fragrance and very flesh of the world.
But you know we're being lied to—
that there is no even hand to pain,
to beauty, to the white blossom
and the promise of dust, quick
in all our days—always, the coils of rain,
and only the simple light
shot out of the heart heads home . . .

When I sit quietly at dusk and look
for the after-glimmer the wind brings
off the water, lifting
the trees' heads skyward, my grandfather
is not the cold alphabet of his name
nor the marker set, nor the mind's eye closed—
he is a brilliant coin of violet light
guiding over my left shoulder,
a voice rising each morning in the east,
the hands I remember
lifting me up into the day . . .
the same voice I hear off the Pacific
that does not long for the body of the world,
a voice that tells me to believe finally
in the rain easing, in the one
water-drop desiring nothing more
than to wear smooth a spot in the stone
and give back its portion of the light.

Why I'm In Favor Of A Nuclear Freeze

Because we were 18 and still wonderful in our bodies,
because Harry's father owned a ranch and we had
nothing better to do one Saturday, we went hunting
doves among the high oaks and almost wholly quiet air . . .
Traipsing the hills and deer paths for an hour,
we were ready when the first ones swooped—
and we took them down in smoke much like the planes
in the war films of our regimented youth.
                                        Some were dead
and some knocked cold, and because he knew how
and I just couldn't, Harry went to each of them and,
with thumb and forefinger, almost tenderly, squeezed
the last air out of their slight necks.
                                  Our jackets grew
heavy with birds and for a while we sat in the shade
thinking we were someone, talking a bit of girls—
who would "go," who wouldn't, how love would probably
always be beyond our reach . . . We even talked of the nuns
who terrified us with God and damnation. We both recalled
that first prize in art, the one pinned to the cork board
in front of class, was a sweet blond girl's drawing
of the fires and coals, the tortured souls of Purgatory.
Harry said he feared eternity until he was 17, and,
if he ever had kids, the last place they would go would be
a parochial school.
                  On our way to the car, having forgotten
which way the safety was off or on, I accidentally discharged
my borrowed 12 gauge, twice actually—one would have been Harry's
head if he were behind me, the other my foot, inches to the right.
We were almost back when something moved in the raw, dry grass,
and without thinking, and on the first twitch of two tall ears,
we together blew the ever-loving-Jesus out of a jack rabbit
until we couldn't tell fur from dust from blood . . .

                                                    Harry has
a family, two children as lovely as any will ever be—
he hasn't hunted in years . . . and that once was enough for me.
Anymore, a good day offers a moment's praise for the lizards
daring the road I run along, or it offers a dusk in which
yellow meadowlarks scrounge fields in the grey autumn light . . .
Harry and I are friends now almost 30 years, and the last time
we had dinner, I thought about that rabbit, not the doves
which we swore we would cook and eat, but that rabbit—
why the hell had we killed it so cold-heartedly? And I saw
that it was simply because we had the guns, because we could.

Heaven Knows

Robinson walking in the park, admiring the elephant.
—*Weldon Kees*

Wednesday, the last of October,
and it's about to rain . . .
The sky is cloud-spun, ashen,
the workings of a cocoon.
I sit secure beneath thick loquat leaves
and it begins lightly in the garden
on cactus and pistachio trees.
The incinerator gives up its last ghosts
and the paired doves fly off the wire.
And there's the woman by her window,
alluring as these lilacs in rain—
she's dreaming on a white moon of cares,
or perhaps the blue evening yet to come.
Her name is Leslie or Kathleen,
there's a Mozart chorale on the phonograph,
and there must be glasses of chardonnay,
the hint of gardenias in the room . . .
I light a cigarette and recall lips, breasts,
the long gold or auburn hair,
and it's no small treasure to remember
even the least part of love
when rain falls lightly through an afternoon.

By Five, the horizon lifts, half the sun
wavers with an amber rose above the fence,
the newspaper arrives with our failures.
I could heat some soup, put the last
zinnias in a water glass on the sill,
but this hour's for red wine and bread,
the cold brilliance at your skin.

My other neighbor has been grinding
on something in his garage—a high whir
builds and fades like this morning's ambitions.
I look to my hands and admire them—
"Nice looking for a man's," she once said,
and so I don't know that this day isn't
only lightly fettered to some eventuality,

a silver maple leaf stalling in a current,
wind-blind before the ground.
Whatever it is I'm doing this day,
it's somehow noted in the long outline
of the air, in time with the jostled quince leaves,
the remaining tumbleweeds of clouds.
I'm left to deal with myself
and the spare content of elements
sustained as they are by rain, by the gradual
appreciation of the daylight for the dark.

I'm without lovers, agents or an Alfa Romeo
and not unlike the perfect fool
happy with that threadbare song,
The Best Things In Life Are . . . etc.
Soon enough I'll succeed, warmly
in an elegant hotel, smile with a gimlet
in a well-meaning sports jacket.
But today, there's the deep
and patient breathing of these trees,
my old coat and basic considerations.

All I want now is this apricot light
dusting down, my heart to settle so,
simple, yet ambivalent as rain.
Evening will roll out its ink
and compose my praise for me, my love . . .
first stars glistening in the water-pockets,
in my eyes, and I'll wait
for the constellations I can name
to blink on above the high persimmon boughs
and the last silver bark of clouds—
I'm as wingless as these branches
bare with rain, anchored as the hours
to our loss and counting. Heaven knows
how long I can sit here before
drifting off, beyond the bright
adornments of this earth . . .

for Jon and Omar

Dust Light, Leaves

Above autumn's burgundy and rust,
beyond the orange groves
chafing and ruddy in the frost,
a cloud lifts into blue . . .
the west goes up all haydust, flame,
and the flat land glimmers
out to it on the day-stream—
it is Millet's sky of "The Angelus,"
that nineteenth-century sky
we have only in paintings
and in these few still moments
in their rose and amber rags.

As a child, I remember this . . .
standing on the creek stones,
dusk moving over the fields
like a ship's hull pulling away
with that first sense of loss
and release; I saw it was
all about the beginning of dust
rising into the long sky's seam,
into my own two eyes and hands.

A chalk-white moon overhead
and to the right, umber waves
of sparrows back and through
the empty trees . . .

Soon, stars will draw analogies
in the dark, but now the world
is simple as the dead leaves
glowing in this late hour,
simple as our desire
to rise lucent as clouds
in their camisoles of dust,
the cool air burning through us
over leaves drifting on a pond,
over the last memory
of ourselves looking up,
stunned as carp blinking at the light.

Five Small Meditations
On Summer And Birds

and it isn't a question, then, of how we feel,
but of how we hold ourselves out to the dark
                              —Sherod Santos

First evening after daylight-saving time
and the past is once again behind me,
everything thrown-by in the sea's blank hands,
in silence and the sky's slow burn. The boats
out late on the glass and glimmer are soon
as vague as a line of brown pelicans
skimming beyond the cove, far and sunward . . .
And now I feel forgotten in the days
and stare as if I'd been warmed by longing.
Now, beneath the eroded cliffs and dead-
gold trees of summer, it seems natural
to wonder about all those I have loved,
adrift on this dust light, that bluest edge
with night always rising—who thinks of me?

A child, I was taken with the unlocked
sweep and chance of wings, the grace of angels
come long after the lift and aim of birds.
Were we purer, we would have seen them part
of what we knew, or were—airy templates,
first glow we gave up and were taken in . . .
Even the towhee with his one poor note,
with ardor in his supplications, says
he's never sure—I try to think as well
what I've said past the basic prayer to say?
I recall a redbird on the farm, bright
in the bronzed poplars—I am four or five
and for all I know he's songless; it seems
enough—float and pause, air to branch to air . . .

God could forget . . . this comes to mind each time
I wake to doves who know sorrows they are
unable to put by. The bloodstone sun,
the dust that sends the west up like neon
on a marquee, gives us a despair hung

irrevocably at hand . . . Already,
God could be unthinking the future—there
we'd each be a little less than the haze,
drifts in days without names, and then we can
say whatever we will about the past . . .
The moon's last eclipse for years, and I saw
then the numinous Milky Way, and thought,
out here, on the light's smudged edge, who ever
could love us best among each shining thing?

Mornings of fog, the grey weight of nothing
new like a wet coat on your shoulders—still,
what reason to hold your heart out to loss?
The temptation is to feel it's useless
to know, *time isn't what it used to be,*
and beneath the wing-drag of hours to lose
patience for the burn-through and vibrato . . .
But then a man turns toward pity, toward old
notes and the weak thinking in his desire,
while the roads won't sigh even a little
for the lost—everything perishable
in the air's web . . . He turns toward a late sun
that gives back the contemplative trees and
the half-songs and enterprise of finches . . .
What did we start with that we don't have now?

Yet even loss glows, gleam and salt of it,
the many things past knowing—so maybe
midnoon is as far back as I need go,
the sparrows congratulating themselves
with water at the birdbath, unburdened
from the wind's lists—I'm not sure they saw me
there, they just seemed to know they were sparrows
in the good summer air, dodging the jays,
cleaning their beaks along the heavy boughs,
untroubled by the conditions of love
or their measure in this world—they gave out
leisure's least praise while drying quietly
in the trees, but left a good deal unsung
to surmount this evening's long sting of light.

Quotidiana

for Charles Wright

Though winter shuffles off in its old coat,
and the incinerator's deliberations go mute in ash,
though the bee-winged blossoms of pyracantha
lift the morning in a butter-white blur,
and the geranium makes its first red move
against the garden stones,
                              and monarchs stall
with sun-streams in the eucalyptus leaves
while you, you wander through the unattended field
saying, *nasturtium, oxalis, sweet alyssum,*
praising the lost children of the wind,

the parish church will ring out The Angelus at 6:00
and the feckless daylight will dismiss
the Courthouse towers as if they were no more
than the palms or pines,
                              and even when violet mists
swim down the foothills of the Santa Ynez,
and the bell grows so thin, so distant,
that you see to the end of a cobbled street
where the last shadow of a cloud drifts
across a duomo in Florence, say, or in Peru,
it will always come back to this—
                              late evening,
before a lamp or star comes on the hill,
the final bird, a dart in the plum-rust light—
late evening, the moment for your answer and again
in the thin shirt of this life you have none—
late evening, one calla lily leaning west,
the heart a dark wash and lost truth,
the world going to one knee.

At Laguna Blanca, Santa Barbara

As if the past
had no purchase on the light
     and the degree
of our omissions would not always be
     as blind
as the stems of a winter field,
     flowerless
and unmendable before wind,

     and as if that wind
didn't unstring the parched fan palms
     of their dust
each time I walk the horse paths here,

     I return
for this blank surface which softens
     even the Spanish clouds
brooding forever above this town—
     I come again
for the solace and clean slate.

     I've stood here often
with the sun-flayed eucalyptus
     and have not
distressed the hundred dreaming birds
     paused between
the shadows and ambered twigs of light,
     just as now
they are untroubled by my desire
     to be this breeze
quitting in the leaves and reeds.

     And how simple here
to admire how the birds care little
     for what they leave behind
and float out frankly as if they knew
     nothing of another life,
the implicit rains, the easy sorrows
     of this one.

Gliding across the glassy lake
    their cloudlike hearts
take up the wind's lost thoughts—
    and now the blue
willows, the burning oaks have me wishing
    that I'd never wished
and could face the darkness unbothered
    as these birds
who return to it without gloss or pity
    and who wake
each day in a new world with nothing
    to be forgiven.

The Roadrunner

for Glover Davis

Hawks take long strides on the wind, and finches
flit blissfully among hibiscus and orange,
a mockingbird recites his ten lies and darts away—
of course these birds tell us something of ourselves

who sit envying their easy passing through
the world, or who, daily now, run ourselves
down the road to clear a glaze of drinks and dinner
from the thick and rounded corners of our frames . . .

So far, we haven't toned to the tight machines,
are not precise, and whatever moves we once possessed
on the fields or courts fade to legends, ancient wars,
and we are worn men turning home, slow boats at sea . . .

After the lifting and the miles only our spirits aspire;
our body heat waves sunward, but we are still over-
generous in our appreciation of this life, and surely
several incarnations from that ascetic plate of self-denial.

With their renunciation of earthly fruits and splendors
St. Raymond of Penafort sailed his cape over the waters,
St. Francis and St. Martín de Porres rose routinely
above the ground . . . at best, our words find form,

some discipline our hearts can take. And they have said
we're men of "bearing," but really it's more "bear-like,"
and I couldn't help but feel so recently one day
in the desert, as I watched a roadrunner crossing

a wide, flat fairway with something considerable
in his beak, feet padding for all he was worth—and,
at the last instant, confronting the boundary fence,
he flapped his mostly inadequate wings, cleared it

without elegance, and was gone in the spare, lush shade.
So who then's to say what part of grace desire finally is,
the prayer of one foot winged or weary before the other?
And may we be as admirable and accomplished by the end.

Work & Days   —at Bonny Doon, Santa Cruz, California

for Gary Young

Mornings, spired shafts of sunlight waver, and you
almost see a hovering of angels' wings above redwood
and pine—angels who must have stood up straight inside
my friend's thin frame and sung as he hoisted out
the creekbed rock to rebuild a chimney and retaining wall,
and all the rest he thinks he did entirely on his own.

Even water loses its breath over the little falls,
ferns and blue hydrangeas drift in primeval shade—
when daylight does flood through, it is fundamental
as our desire, and no matter how disaffected you are
with God, it is clear then that time is something
that keeps only in the loosening of our bones . . .

And so our hands' slow work, this waste and sweetness
of the days, of the heart's implicit praise, content
to let the future find us as it will—in a garden pool,
the carp sift brilliantly among their moss as we compare
the lines of our faces, lines crossed in our palms,
realizing there is no good luck, really, no bad.

We could almost be older men, we drink our beers
so quietly, breathing our lives out into thin clouds
which gather on the cold and dusk—it is then we lean
back on our benches or stand to catch the evening's
final shift through the trees, like a last glimpse
of angels' robes, slightly soiled with their care here.

La Strada

for Cheryl

Again today, the unassuming clouds,
and, as if I had a prayer,
I let some wish go out on them
in their distracted devotion to the sky—
then, in a book as gold and brittle as winter leaves,
I came across something I've always known:
in Italian, *Gelsomina* means *jasmine* . . .
and so I saw then the white and antic blossom
of her face, so much like yours,
and for the moment it rose shining above
the narrow roads and straw of earth.

And I wanted to tell you that our dreams,
which are surely dust, are still our dreams,
and what little we can ever make of them
will save us for a while, even as the bonfires
suggest our fates in their bright thorns and smoke.

Perhaps you can recall the coast of Gaeta,
a little violin, the high, wistful music
and the cavatinas of the nuns, or someone
walking past laundry drying late in a breeze
who is stopped by that small tune as it is bowed
sorrowfully off the clouds, off the salt and foam
with their sting of absence? Perhaps someone
like Zampano, hung-out in the fading days,
in his brute skin, in some dead husband's suit . . .

I remember a moon there in the evening sky
and your face with its own unconscious luster—
and when I've turned to the sea with its lost arms,
or to the old roads blanched with time,
it has always followed just over my shoulder . . .

And I remember you in your cape, bird-like
across the yard, pecking the wind's palm for your fortune,
fretting about the fool who took half your pain
and disappeared with stars into the dawn river . . .

Now, returned to your parent's house
where the lantern in your father's chest sputters
its last colors to the night, where work is empty,
as endless as the tide, it might help to know this,
might make the loveless reaches a degree less dark—
Gelsomina/jasmine: white petal of the soul,
one song along this unavowed path of sorrows.

Postcard From Italy

Hours south of Milano, of Ortona, south
of Foggia and Barletta, past Bari and
Polignano a Mare, south where the train
quits its stops as frequent and abrupt
as the ends of Latin sentences, a red soil
rises up through Fasano and Villanova,
and with the evening, rolls endlessly as far
as Brindisi—you see it forcing its way
up the limbs of the olive trees and out
into the terra cotta cast of an old light
thick in the unguent leaves, thicker yet
in the grapes, dark and sagging toward
the wine-end of August; and a rose dust
dropping in a skein over the disced fields
becomes as familiar as the inflections
on the ancient language that you speak now,
if only silently, to yourself, or to the blue
shag of the olive barks, the blank standards
of the dead who lift softly from this
stained ground as the night lets down
its steep ladders—and alone or not alone,
you can't help but make their voices out
each time the train slows through another
unmarked village, by another broken wall
of stones all the way to the Adriatic . . .

Insomnia

Half a moon and again
awake with all the aimless
absolutes of worry,
not the least of which
is the light from any star
which could already be dead . . .
Recently, a friend pointed to stars
and said *Draco, the dragon.*
I could make out nothing,
but someone had a reason
to make a disconnected line
of lights that looked like nothing,
something—some sleepless gazer
giving order in an older world . . .

Tonight, I'm heavily at sea
in this one—money and mail,
digestion or the heart,
all the too usual particulars
of a grey that sinks you here
to the desk, to postcards,
and Greece is popular again this year.
One writes from Santorini, Thera:
Aegean, extraordinarily beautiful—
Minoan city destroyed by a volcano
circa 1,500 B.C.—met an Englishman
who knew Jack Gilbert here—I'm feeling
for once relaxed, almost calm . . .
Another saying: *Summertime in Mykonos—*
canvas awnings of tavernas shading
walks—the painted fishing skiffs,
the hot, white horizons, and no one
hurries to anything far into the night—
along the water there seem to be
more stars than at home—twice we have
seen someone who we were sure was you . . .

The buildings, shell white, saint white,
ascend the ancient rocks—dreams
outdistanced, some other life . . .
And how appropriate, this half moon—
Old Testament Jews thought it out,
and the stars too: pulleys across a vault,
leak-throughs and crusts of light,
always something on the other side,
always the grasping in the dark.
                                        Still,
no specific reason for malaise,
just the stalled landscape
repeating heat until sleep
too is a foreign country . . .
but not one in which we drink
or sit at tables desiring
the women who pass
beautifully through the afternoons,
or need something else to say,
but that one in which we take
a windless passage to islands,
bay to bay on air-blue water,
where by night the thousands
of small and luminous fish
skim peacefully just below
the moonlit, starlit surface.

for David Wojahn

III

Prayer

Even though birds always take the air
in the perfect attitude of their wings,
even though grace and fate are afterthoughts
and there is only one song, flying—
they turn home heavier and half-empty
for the night, and, nestled among blue leaves,
offer some last phrase for the future . . .

This afternoon I am out
to prune the oleanders, the shocks of white
duplicitous flowers, the leaf-blades ribboning
the sun's way here . . . Always it seems,
we have our reasons. But soon,
swaying on one leg, the aluminum ladder
elbowed by wind, I am asking
forgiveness of the robins and doves,
taking the hedge down to a bundle of sticks,
as if our backs or theirs were ever wanting . . .

Love, if you were here now,
or somehow we could speak after all
the trouble our hearts and the years have been,
I would say only how purely the clouds pass,
taking the world in, letting it go
effortlessly, more lovely than ourselves,
almost our own coefficient of the birds
as they take a pebble in their beaks
for ballast—one more mote of the past—and fly
songless, a little to the south . . .
I think how I'd like to be unpuzzled
as the birds, as compromising and unconcerned,
better than I am.

On A Photograph Of Monet
In His Garden At Giverny

Autumn breaking through the willow leaves, and arced
trellises empty to a sky as opaque as final nymphaeas,
white across the water-garden. Head-high with daisies,
with rose canes listing toward winter, you're of a kind
here, composed in a suit of mossy tweeds, only barely
distinguished among the still and thickening greens.

With a fedora pinched low against this day-slant
and your hermit's beard unconscious as any cloud,
it's hard to tell how you've admired the haystacks
hunkered in the west field haze, burning there, rouged
with that longing at day's end, almost pendant as wisteria
hanging from the footbridge in the violet summer sky.

You've grown fastidious about the atmospheres, the half-
moons of light, and sense the sky pulling finally away
with its gold and pink, reissuing a collective loss—
behind you, the gravel walk is worn as smooth, as grey
as every truth about the past—that sift of lavender
silt always edging the shiftings in your sight . . .

Your shoes are shined—a serious man, you modestly enjoy
a smoke by the spines of hollyhock, pausing perhaps
to recall the high, lost music of that air they are
climbing still, and thereby learn more of what it is
to disappear, to sag with the stiff leavings of Fall
and discover yourself a fit subject for a photograph.

And so, with the dark and bat wings early in the trees
you may now only care to consider your spare engravings
from the Japanese—the immaculate breasts of two women
washing in the estuary; a quiet snow capping the deep
and formal waves; lanterns of the bath house blooming
like bright petals above the blue and aqueous night.

for Nadya and Jon

Munch's "Harvesting Women"

The afternoons are thick and baggy
as our suits, and whether we look
to the sky for a dove of purpose
or to the ground after something fallen,
there is little more than the thinning bark
going gold in the day's last dusty minutes,
chipping away like promises
made by lovers we cannot recall.
What is an old man in summer
but a tree relieved of every burden
and still leaning? Grass browning
in green wind, ready to tangle
in the sticks of his own bones?
What we know now are these women
in their flower-white dresses, the fruit
high and far we can no longer reach . . .
As they are busy about the lower limbs
the peach-ripe sun blooms on
their arms and faces—our hands
weigh in our pockets like lifeless quail,
and we're only out to take the air.

Diffidence

for S.A.S.

I sit in one of the dives
On Fifty-second Street
Uncertain and afraid . . .
Auden

Diffidence of heart—that's the cliché,
shyness and a reticence to speak;
but I'm offering nothing so genteel.
Rather, the worn valves and spinners in the clock,
the early wondering about the winding down,
which can as easily crimp the spirit,
blank some frames midway in the long run.

Drinking beer in some place cool,
dark beneath the level of the street,
I've found the leisure pulse of afternoon,
and though our music's out of sync,
I nevertheless drum out a little praise
to the leaves and intemperate birds,
to the spry and festooned season.
And through the high window
a skirt sashays and light sparkles
off the blowing cottonwoods as if off water,
the clear eyes of those who drink it—
I lean back and salute the living . . .

With the slightest suggestion from the Muzak
I'm humming *April In Paris* and thinking years ago—
there were no chestnuts in blossom
or holiday tables under the trees, but,
as effortlessly as Mel Tormé, we were
up and down the boulevards . . .
                              At night,
in a lavender shirt and leather jacket,
you're smoking Gauloises, meticulously,
chasing the vin ordinaire with a beer,
and watching the bistro lights blink off,
the whores giving up, the dog-eyed waiter
with the usual curse for lingerers.

Life was all in the pronunciation,
no further away than a stage railing
where strippers named for exotic flowers
unfolded perfectly, petal by slow, ripe petal.

There were women of course,
hard times without them.
Hangovers were mild and the sun
dovetailed into your attic room
as you ran croissants and café au lait
up the hotel stairs and now you think,
how simple a thing to stay alive. Sometimes,
old bread, only enough for a grappa
and the blustery afternoon light
scattering ashes in the glass.
But all this through an amber lens,
and were we unhappy then?

Once, predictably, in the Eiffel Tower,
I was drinking with Jean from Chicago,
and in the rose light and glow of my blood
I was confident I could see clear
to the Sacré-Coeur. For an hour I felt
complete as that evening light,
immutable as the gold and perfect hills . . .

Friend, the long evenings are here,
the ineluctable sifting of violet skies—
the gin and tonic, the ice and lime,
the litany when someone should pause to say,
This is gracious living, something we deserve.
And on these flagging afternoons
we wish, but know there's no way to go back,
no one to look for us where we walked
a path toward fading light and blue shadow,
the stars blearing above the dream.

We're told. These ceremonies have to go.
And we'll drink to Paris, Ireland, or nothing
never again. And it will be from across the street
we'll notice the beaten run of daylight rust
in the patina of the barroom glass.

Now, after an afternoon of work,
before the dinner and company at Seven,
we face the inexorable hour of Four o'clock,
its tide of nerves that rankles down the arm.
It needs a little something
to buff the edge off the absolute,
the plain beauty or pain always in the way,
roses you must arrange and not admire.
There's soda but no brandy, no smokes,
the conscious problem of sleep,
the thinking back and the fear of the dark.
We'll see how adamant our hearts become
and if we can hold out an affirming flame.

Save Yourself

after Carlos Drummond de Andrade

Chris, my friend, be patient,
it takes little to wait . . .
You have done some work,
there will always be more.
And the Sundays will arrive
but just as certainly the Thursdays,
the long afternoons with their one rock,
two rocks, piled just so . . .
God too was younger when you began—
life is short, so now
no more knots in the rope.

Consider the parable of wheat,
or the sower, the mustard seed—
the sparrows whose work is never done,
who sing for nothing as their reward—
forget about the tall stone jars of wine,
think only of the water,
how it gives back
your face without remorse.
Stop doing yourself in
with cigarettes, newspapers,
the blue arguments of stars . . .

The apple of your heart is green,
it spoils you for the dance,
for the well-meaning women,
those who sit at your table to drink,
those who do not—of all people,
who are you to judge a blessing?

Save yourself for that girl
poised modestly in a doorway
of a narrow street, the frail dark one
stepping into sunlight
after a morning's rain,
lifting her veil a little to look
up the hill toward the campanile
and long necklace of clouds,

to look, perhaps, into your face,
in that village, on that island
you may visit a year from now—
perhaps nothing of the kind,
but calm down, imagine the names
long into the evening—
Teresa, Cybele, Margarete . . .

And throw your father's revolver
into the sea, but don't listen
to the doves sorrowing there
along the strand—also,
give no thought to the waves
with their garlands of salt
for the worn, for the lost,
or the cypresses always leaning
a little in that direction . . .

And be careful in August
when festivities move outside—
keep your back to the moon,
and smiling politely
in your white summer jacket,
be the true romantic
and call for another tango
from the accordion player,
the dancers will feel appreciated,
your hosts will congratulate themselves,
then refuse another gin and lime,
eat a little and turn in
before the headache and the dawn.

Chris, my boy, have some hope.
Most of the time, love is a small
silver bell about a finch's throat,
and by night it's always sounding
far and away, no, nearby—nevertheless,
you've seen the cities and the cliffs
below, you've seen things
shine before . . . and yet tonight,
worn out with the old desires,
you're ready to give in
to the useless drums and mandolins,
the insomnia of clouds.

                              Be reasonable.
Turn to the bedside and put out
the lamp, drink from the easy glass
of sleep . . . Save yourself, tomorrow
observe the indifference of cottonwoods
to wind, the evening light that sings
through the arabesques of leaves.
Then remember your guitar,
what a dull thing misery is.
Save yourself, for surely somewhere
things are written down,
and it all will change, a little,
sooner or later—you can count on it.
Be patient. There is no one
who does not tire pushing
his little cart of troubles along,
and no one will inherit the earth.
Think of your friends
who are living too—save yourself.

Snow

Again today, I feel that I have loved too little
and never well enough, for in these myopic afternoons
no music lifts from backyards or patios alongside

purple bougainvillaea, and no lovers await evening
from a veranda—and though I can recall the professor's
lissome wife, the precise volcanic red of geraniums

she whispered to on her portico, and even the burning
scent of the orange trees in her hair all that winter
in Cuernavaca, I cannot remember exactly how it was

I found it necessary to leave, only to return to this
middling state with birds dismissed from the chestnut trees
and little more in my hands than this embarrassed guitar,

warping and one string short, fit only for the wind
to play through its center, thin as the air's memory
of the birds' long flight, no love song at all . . .

And thoroughfares are thick with silence, its lost breath,
so dream or not dream, it is the same now, the heart is
no more than an oak leaf falling in the frozen garden,

the street lamp going blind in the intermittent drifts.
Here is the unimaginable heart of nothing, my hand melting
its clear, starred shape into the frosted windowpane.

And like these trees that have let go all their wishes,
I am here despite all of mine, save one in the unknown
animal's tracks slipping carefully past the porch,

or in a glass of Spanish sherry held skyward, west
where I'd be home, with swallows and blue air swarming
up from Baja, with yellow apples invisibly beginning

in the bright mountains of Santa Cruz—my old friend
wandering through his small orchard there, praising
the white hosts of blossoms, working in poles beneath

clouded boughs already bent a little in anticipation
of sap humming up the heartwood, and the light's
final push out the limbs into our ever faithful arms.

for Ken & Susie Smith in Murray

Spring And The Half Life

I

Each spring the wind up this hill
takes me by the back of the neck
as if I were still lacking
a little something in the world,
as if I'd again stammered out,
a boy daydreaming over his lesson,
a passage he never adequately explains.

Already, I've taken too much time
deliberating the heart-slide of a week ago,
the blossoms and the bones
of our days held up before us
mutable as any leaf, and simply how
we want to last longer than the trees.
Learning from them, I stand here patiently
turning over the only phrase I recall
about the passing and the glory of the world.

II

All around me now
the fields offer up oxalis, poppy, lupin,
the calla lilies' essential white,
and it's natural to sense the lush
and frantic push to life,
especially if as a child you were marched
in a pressed collar and polished brown shoes
to chorus an "O Salutaris Hostia"
to the visible and invisible spheres.
And though Sister Caritas assured us
we would find singing and a place of favor,
a spring downpour and thunder taught us
fear even in the flowering of our arms.

By the time I was 20 I'd forgotten
all the infinite arrangements, until
one day in May, in a square in Seville,
I was feeding pigeons that balanced
heavily along my forearm and wrist,

but at the sounding of the tour bus horn
they lifted in one awkward shake
like an old blanket being emptied
of its winter dust, and I was alone
my hand held empty toward the light,

III

Today, I think of the pigeons Picasso sketched
at 9, how he had them perch instinctively
on next to nothing, a line or two in space . . .
and I remember seeing him close to 90
with that ardor renewed in the very thought
of birds, their airy source and grace
almost palpable there in his hands . . .
And today, I am also thinking of Corot,
his landscapes and atmospheres—for instance,
the painting at Ariccia, the church walls
resonant in the half-life of afternoon,
and above the little woods and sticks of earth
the mists of light angled and rising for us
toward that unknowable portion of the sky.

And so my hope becomes that slight glimmer
windswept above the failing blue,
above the unconscious luster, which by night
seeps down to us and restores the small
white star beneath our collarbones—
and then, perhaps, we glide out
through the glass, glowing in procession
above the blooming trees, the starry fields,
and glimpse there the idea of the world
apart from the world itself, or our love
without any one thing to love—what we are
when we are no longer what we are.

Zurbaran's "Still Life: Lemons, Oranges And A Rose" 1633

The lemons are brilliant, implicit
as the halo of the silver plate,
as their lines, like saints' fingers
in older paintings, pointing skyward . . .

The oranges are gold, quintessentially so,
and burn fervently with their basket
in the day-slant—their green leaves
catch and hover, the small clouds
of blossoms seem to dissolve and lift away . . .

To the right, another plate, a cup of water
and one rose half the color of our blood,
or a woman's skin never exposed to sun—
they edge the darkened background
with all the melancholy in desire . . .

In less than a year he will die,
this the last still life he will paint—
the St. Francis and St. Lawrence are done,
gone into their long, mystic gazes . . .

And so, just out of view, high to the left,
he has opened his last window to the evening,
to a world clearly ordered for the light . . .

Resting on this plain wood table,
these common objects rise,
ardent in this final realm—
the earth transcendent without us.

IV

Smoke

(For The Poets Of Spain)

the top leaves
are green smoke dreaming far away.
—*Machado*

From cobwebs I cull flowers.
So I use my grief.
—*Hernandez*

The soft coal of dreams is burning—
the trestle and the train go up with you
grey as the last bud of powder from the war,
grey as the ash-blessed clouds.
You stepped in that river and were gone—
salt rubbed from the palms,
blood into the sand of Granada.
Years in the shadow of it all
and we sometimes see
feathers of light fluttering
over the earth's hard edge
and know the world gives up a little
each day in your loss—
gives up like the granite
in Valle de Los Caidos
like the fists of loyalists
forced to cut that granite
in the images of saints
who were looking the other way.
The soft coal of dreams is burning . . .

Those who have gone before us,
in the middle of their road,
are paper doves into the sea.
The days throw down their fortune
to this one and overlook the other,
but we all have our shirts, shoes.
Our vision is a frank one
and in the imagined hills
there is no white mare nuzzling
the fine gold apples of the moon.
Rather, we see ourselves a horse
like any other, plodding in our love,

hauling our cart of sticks in winter
across a bridge, praying
as evenly as the agave climbs
flower to flower out of itself
toward some sustaining air, toward
those who have gone before us.

Who am I that I should ask
who will arrive beyond the bones
of his hands, sufficiently humbled
when they fold the coats of the dead?
I began blindly in the church,
in the candles mirrored in tin—
our life not of this world, but in it.
We threw ashes on each heart,
fed each fruit of remembrance,
and so the past is our grief and our rose,
a lantern held wonderingly before us, asking,
who am I that I should ask?

We are by most accounts still young,
but over our shoulder
we can feel death's cold breath,
see her hems dragging
through the trees at dusk.
Who would disregard the dull bells
strung to the ankle, and walk,
as you did, beside her with a compliment
for the dry meter of her hands,
the dark birds of her arms?
Just as you were then,
when that gypsy pulled her knife,
we are by most accounts still young.

Each of us carefully banks the fire.
To reduce the wing-flap in our pulse
we begin to only speak of wine,
and when a flame-blue burns over tamarisks
at 8:00, we run the avenues,
along train tracks and see the cloud
from the engine's stacks drift and spindle
before the oil seeps to the lung;
I count with the heartbeat paying out
like a merchant dropping coins,
one by one into his purse.

There are dark blood-spots
lodged somewhere in the flesh
like moths waiting for our eyes—
each of us carefully banks the fire.

Until we are as you are,
a white ivy of dreams above the blue,
and say exactly what it is we love
in last straws of light on cirrus clouds,
it must be enough to hold two hands up
and command the ground between—
love what we will, the clouds dissolve,
say what we will, the clouds outlast it.
Part of it is a courtyard and somnambulant moon,
a man oblique down that sleep-blue road,
explaining to someone on a balustrade
how time is the flame put to paper,
how no guitars play in the afterlife,
and how, in between, gardenias turn to wounds.
Far in a dry field of purple thistle
there's a fire and a ladder of smoke
starting up the amber air;
halos of dust circle my feet, my shadow
slips off behind me like water as I run
toward the last grey wisp of light,
until we are as you are.

Poem On A Birthday

Again, the sycamores are empty,
January's haze drifting through.
Again, you linger on this distillate
of earth and air and day-thread.

Wasn't it you who knew
indirections in such a sky
and what to make of clouds?
Now clouds are nothing more than stones
along that oldest road home,
and no matter when the palms bend
or the seabirds calm,
it is still a long way
when you have no idea what to do
with the darkness pooling beneath the trees,
a darkness that, at this time each day,
grows upward from your feet
and makes you wonder how,
standing in one place so long,
you haven't taken up the earth's
doubting waters completely to your heart?

You consider these picked boughs,
your hand held sensibly toward the sun,
the fact that every day you
have five new chances at this life.
You confront the Chinese Elm,
its sloughing bark, your body
lugging, almost loath to begin again.
Gravity is having its way—
and why then hasn't the earth
shrunk to salt, the seas risen
back bluely to the stars, to whatever
was here before us and unnamed?
You thought you'd stacked patience'
last small bone—you had, after all,
these trees, the wooden bowl of your heart
always begging before God, the North Star
against the dark.
            Old leaf, new leaf,
last anything to the wind,

you cannot give in and rest; you must
accept the sand or dust filling your cuffs,
admire the falling stars
and forget they're falling,
while on the horizon, the last branches
bare into a lusterless, blue burn.
This is the life you choose—
what can you do
but keep faith with whatever
turns the light is going to take?
Here is heaven's wheel
and this must be your shoulder.

Ambition

Home from work, the light unthreading itself
through the trees, and again the outline
of the campanile is a wishbone against the blue,
one your best intentions never seem to bend.

And no matter what tune the wind suggests
in the leaves, and, if you muse along or not,
you can afford to wait out the unfinished music
of early stars—and a mockingbird laying claim
to it all, he's going nowhere fast as well.

So at 36 you begin to think it possible
that you never were that discreet romantic
of a Buñuel film, that you never will be
the character of obscure charm your Spanish heart
has always insisted that you are . . .

But without pity, and so far as you know
off camera, you shrug the shoulders
of your seersucker coat and feel improved
as you pull your hands from the pockets
of the matching pants; but the pockets turn out
as if you were proving that you're broke—
very much the way you looked that August
in Madrid, waiting outside Plaza Mayor
for the only woman you knew in town
with silk hose and a black and yellow dress
of polka dots slit clear to there, as she
rode by in an airport taxi, and casually
tossed her cigarette out the window.
Shortly thereafter, you stopped whistling
"The Continental," gave up the guitar;
you returned to the states and a teaching job
and became a reconnoiterer of the young.

And here you are at day's end in this suit,
a well-worn, light and anonymous blue—
"spiffy" they would have said 20 years ago;
skinned, thin with possibility, you think now.

You covet a sports jacket in *Gentlemen's Quarterly,*
are amenable to lunch on the patio,
croquet this afternoon on a barbered lawn—
with dinner, the discretion of an '81 Meursault.

Still you hear your father saying, "Sales.
Why *don't* you go into sales?" as he gleams
in his permanently pressed shirt and slacks,
in his Rolex chronometer worth easily
three times as much as your car—he points out
how many have discovered Real Estate!

Yet, perhaps for a month or two, you might
sell Corvettes in that lot by the beach,
wear loafers, polished cottons, a striped tie
from some college in the east . . . if you sold
but one or two a week you could say, "Yes. Yes
gentlemen; yes in a way to it all."

But the light sifts languidly across the bluffs—
it is almost summer, and there will be little
more to do than you are doing now—*ruminating*
the old poets would have said; *taking it all in*
you'd say—the flamboyant birds of paradise,
the violet immortelles, succulents clutching
their water drops jewel-like as you spray the lawn.
Besides, the heart has its alibi, its recitative
of hope, and all the way to September you are free
to be nonchalant with palms and outriggers drifting
the indeterminate skies of your Hawaiian shirts.

And then later perhaps, in autumn, the inscrutable
mud larks may make sense, and by then you may
value the hapless epigrams and vagaries of clouds,
the grey sidestepping of evening light, and so
become at home with everything that takes you down
a notch as this world goes, each foreclosure of desire
that names you, *laggard, last handler of the wind* . . .

Sparrows

Like the poor, they are with us always . . .
what they lack in beauty is theirs
in good cheer—tails like pump handles
lifting them first among songsters, chiding
citylight or roadside to evening's praise.
Gristmills, hardy gleaners, but for them
the weeds and thorns would find us wanting.
Ragmen to the wind, Sophists of the twig,
they pause to bathe in the ample dust,
and accept the insect as relish to the seed.
So it is becoming to not be too fastidious
when you are rapidly inheriting the earth.

for Gary Soto

Another World War III Dream

Similar to everyone else's
I am alive after the light goes off
somewhere to the north or west of us—
perhaps we've had the foresight
to move to Venezuela or Brazil?

Nevertheless, it's evening,
and there is my family
surrounding a table,
my father going on
about politics and science—
light-years! he declares,
as if his mind has just spanned
the vast troughs of space,
but he has no idea of the cold,
uncountable lifetimes between
stars, or the way Time
may only be hanging on
this cinder in God's great eye,
this quarter note among all the lost
music of a universe . . .
                    Day by day
and from birth we've cherished it,
the dusty slough of time passed
through our blood and breathing,
through the body's thin walls—
this body, above all else,
in and of this world. And so,
we wore the skins of beasts,
lifted rocks, took up a sword
and the very engines of the sun . . .

Looking out to the deep—
blue powder of the night
so indeterminate with its light,
I am reminded that Ptolemy too
had a vision of this earth, centered
among all the celestial motes,
and some way, this same weak thinking
has prevailed . . .

> Now,
> we could each be our own systems
> loosed to meteoric winds,
> a snow of atoms blinking
> across the inscrutable dark—
> and so, perhaps these spheres
> are not so bright or far away
> as we contend—perhaps it's all
> much closer than we think?

Four Stories

Nothing less than winter, the earth
giving up its body to the cold.
Little to say for a life
but the wind goes on saying it . . .
And the thin imagination of the trees
suggests only that the purple martins
are lost to Sarasota or Boca Raton.

And if my soul would quit with its
"Nevertheless," and, "So it came to pass"
I might recall how the chilled stars turn
it cold enough to stop a blowing snow
and how your lungs burn as you suppose
they might climbing a high trail in search
of one of the lost lakes of Switzerland.

In the village you come across
conversation about the first lake
to unfreeze and then disappear,
how it shifts through high meadows
like a thin, blue cloud—but you are
either too early or too late because
no black-necked swans are feeding there
and the wild rose canes spin at the wind's
quick edge, while the only movement
is a ripple of Vs across the surface
mimicking the swans' absent drifting.
It comes down to you and the running
sentences of light buffed off the lake,
the raw silks of clouds untying themselves
from the least suggestion, from winter's
ransom, half-hearted and down wind.

The glass in my study window distorts
the fields to a surface white-capped
with light—and there are times,
casting about for the probable, that I wish
someone would tug at my shirtsleeve

and say where I have lost track. But usually
the sky is gathering its sorrows and rain,
usually the narcissus has not returned
and that's enough for me to stand
along with the retired couple next door
who also cannot overcome the past,
especially the way they stand out there
each day now in the face of the wind
pulling the leaves into souring piles—
and the longer you stand absentmindedly
seeing cares into one form or another,
the more you turn to the color of wind
which never settles anything . . .

Perhaps I could take my good health to Italy—
keep house between Florence and Rome;
perhaps I could consider another interpretation
of light, and along with the birds, feel
no compunction in wishing it from the sky?

Or if I returned to Venice, the Piazza San Marco,
I could sit out the temperate evenings
at a small iron table—a flute of champagne,
sugar wafers for the pigeons; I could even smoke
a cigarette and watch the peach and violet
water-mists lift away beyond the Lido,
and I could love that.
                              And I could step
into church there for the Angelus, for lives
lingering with the incense and the ash,
for the gold mosaics, the way of thorns,
and I could go to one knee and acknowledge
everything—but it may be best not to
call God's attention to myself, our burdens
being relative and likewise our blessings.
Perhaps I should satisfy myself sparrow-like
amid these worn branches, believing
that spring will bring some blossom,
no matter how small or green, how predictably
wind-blown, no matter there or here . . .

And when the rain quits the roads, I might
take one, and with the robins' rusted blurtings
about hope, be little more than I was as a boy,
splashing puddles, happy and full of clouds,
content to gather whatsoever might be luminous
and lifted into life to shine or sound forth
on the boundless air . . .

Or I see myself on beaches in the Yucatan—
the islands of Cozumel and Isla Mujeres where
the white sands have lost sight of time,
where warm, somnambulant waters let a slim boat
of moon drift imperturbably through
the scarlet, equatorial skies, and you
do not have to choose between exotic histories
that birds recount from the inlands
and the amorous breeze in the carnauba palms.

So Roberto Houston, tell me if you will
about the inglorious bones of Nicaragua
and who wept over the rose of Granada,
but do so over here on the patio above the bay,
and bring two tall glasses of something cool
so our old afflictions can drift and become
no more than sobriquets, old news for the winds . . .

Because finally the heart wears weak
as a leaf, and the mind tosses uneasily
in winter, because the wind is a great
repeater, and all its platitudes are ours
for the taking, and because nothing
is ever written on the snow's blank page.
We need, after all, a little dream
to glide out on, some small desire
plotting with the wind how to slip-
stream out toward the pure narration
of that foreign sun.

For A Friend Lacking Faith

Santa Barbara 1983

Here is the hill, and there our city
fading in the celestial summer light—
And now I have nothing to add to the theme
of clouds and our wistful distress,
nothing but the years we climbed here
beneath them, our certainties dimming
as the burnt hems of dusk dragged
the shoreline and went dark in time . . .

But often with our sacks full of clouds
and Spanish champagne, we came to consider
our fates' spun wheel running loose across
the blueprint of the night, and shrugged
our shoulders at the bright inconsequence,
the darkened fields of our going forth.

Now it's November and I'm close to nowhere
in the shallow South. Leaves are falling
orange or gold, and soon every color
will have emptied from the sky and greyed.
And though there are always two glasses
on my table, there are the ineffaceable miles,
the snow winds riding up the back of silence.

Yet there's something to these sleeping fields,
so perhaps we should each put down
our bundle of sticks and take faith
with the milkweed, which is even now preparing
a last song, white and the wordless for the wind—
and likewise wish our wishes gone,
and therefore our sorrows as well . . .

Below your house, the boatlamps wink
with possibility; there are the restaurants
and boulevard, the breakwater and the moon—
those glimmerings no more naming us now
than a little dust red along the footpath down.
And descending so often, I think we have become
steadied on each other's arm, somewhat bent,
but strongly so like the cliff cypresses
with their sinew knotted around air.

I can almost see leaves of oak and acacia,
hear them, dry and rustling in the dark—
and now am reminded of the Japanese, who
fix small bells on temple-garden paths,
the clappers strung with stiff ribbons
to take the least breeze and sound along
so one alone does not lose his way, late
in the evenings as the pines smoke down
the deep plum sky, or, especially by night
as the stars with their bells of light
are sounding too far away to be sure . . .

for Don

As It Is

For Peter Everwine

400 years ago there may have been
wild horses drinking at dusk
from the valley's long white river
and lamps still burning in the glacial stones;
there may not have been, but
we love to feel it was so
each time the day breaks faith with winter
and the wind loses its will
across the yard—each time the milkweed
and chokeberry, miners' lettuce and
tobacco plant call us back
to the tasks of our kind. And each time
I preserve the labor of my hands
and praise equally with my eye—
next to the charity of sunlight
who am I to name thistle or flower?

I pick yellow sour grass and chew
a stem like some boy in school,
and the cool acids bring to mind
the great histories of how we've lived
and died . . . a lark's song fades
seaward toward the Peloponnesos,
in this, another season of our unmaking . . .

Evening comes in her violet robes
and the wild poppies wink out
to the prosody in the night sky—
not that there is all that much to say,
but one wants to get through this life,
our palms turned upward
for the last grey glove of light.
One walks a long way
and finally sits, and is composed,
peaceful with the dust, with the twinge
along the shoulders where wings break
as the first breeze blows in off the stars.

One looks at stars, at the random fields,
one looks to either hand,
lights a cigarette and lets the small
clouds of smoke respond from his fingers
as trees begin their song in the dark.
One wants it as it is,
assured that he can never hold it all.